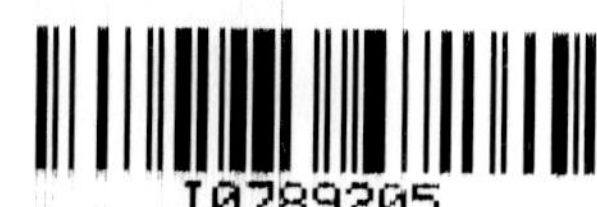
I0789205

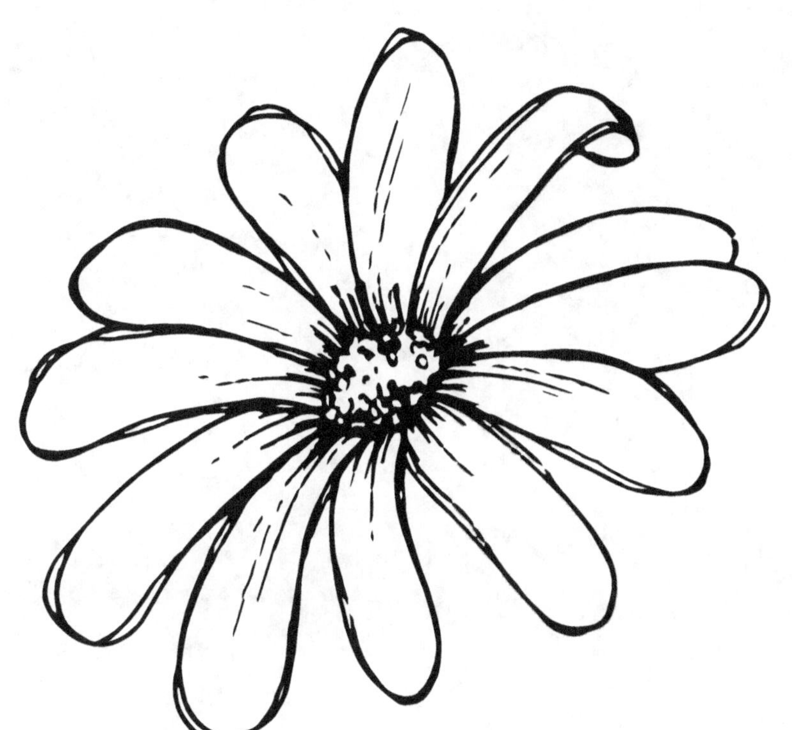

MINIMALIST COLORING BOOK

color, frame & hang

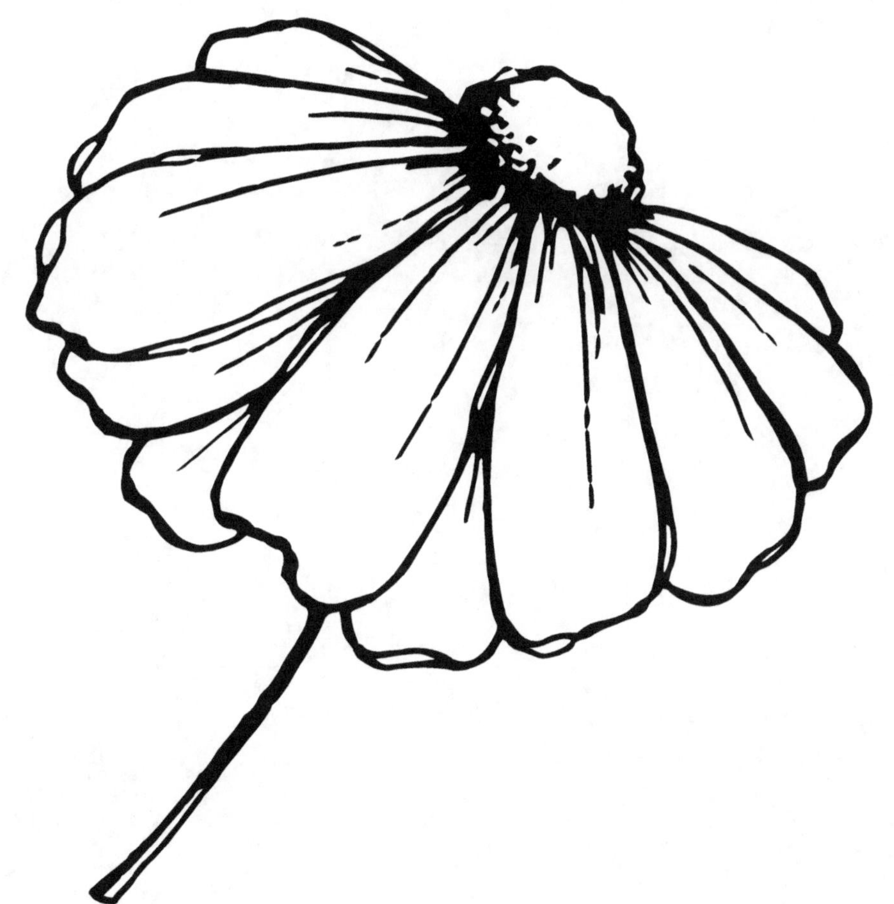

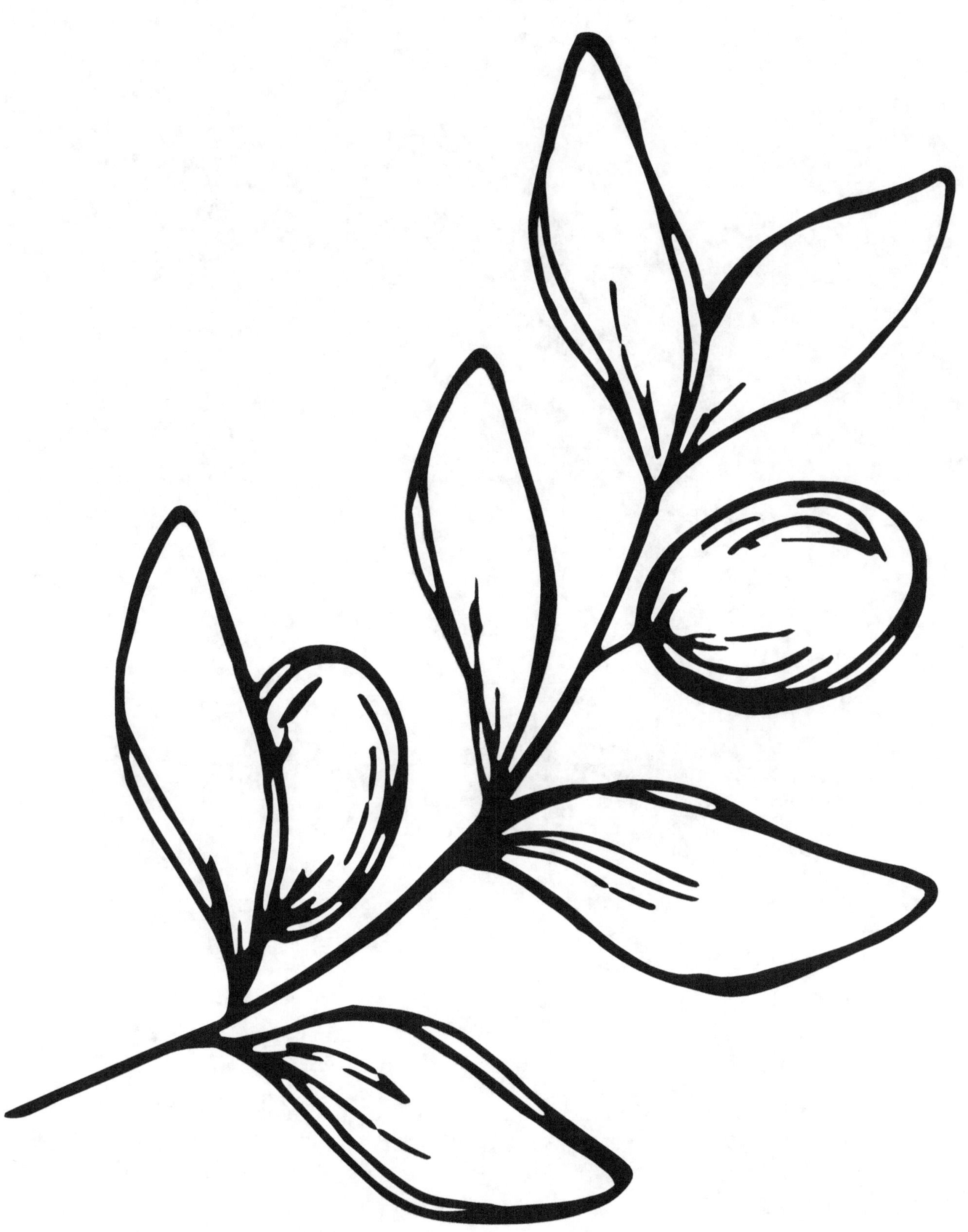

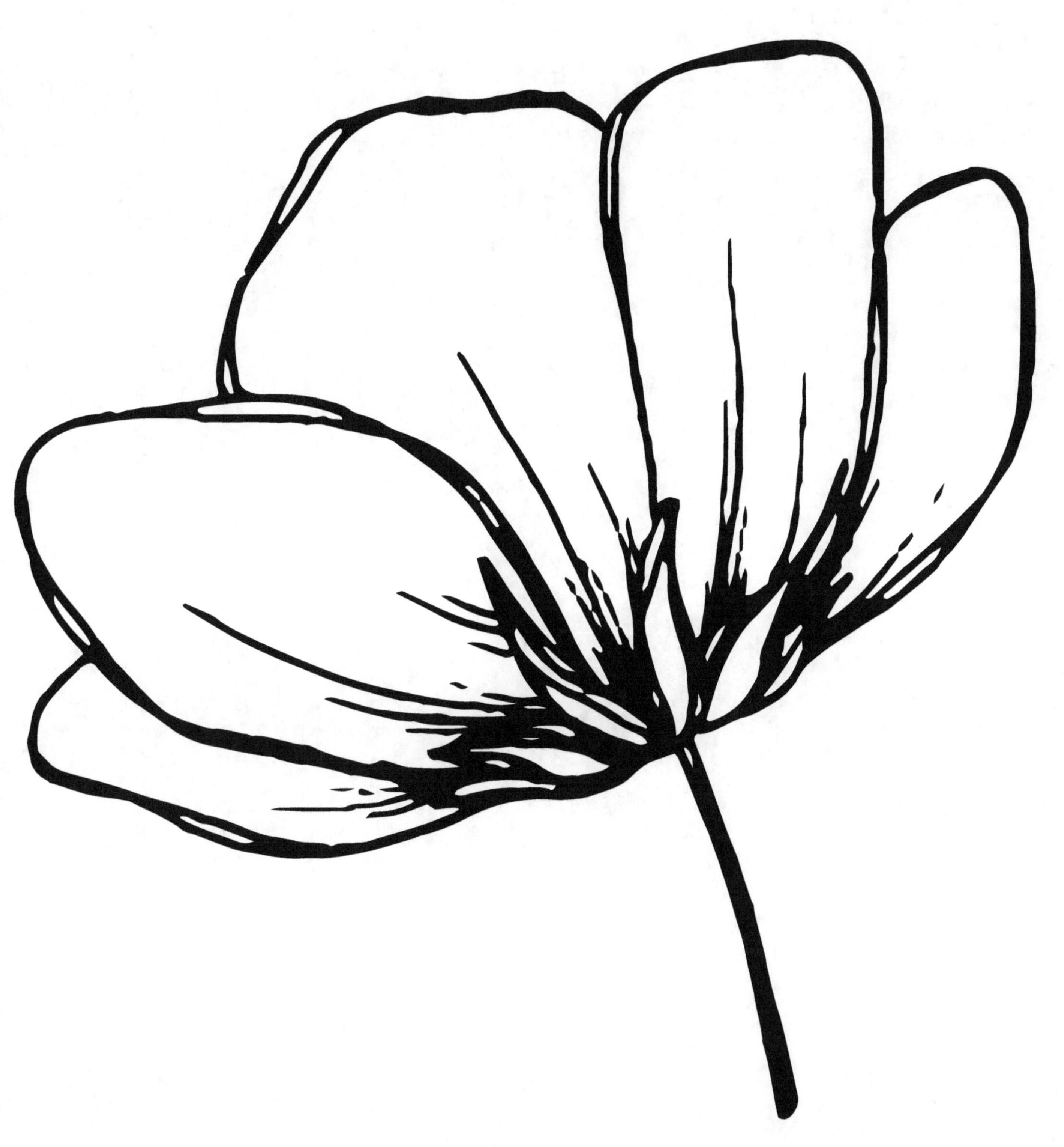

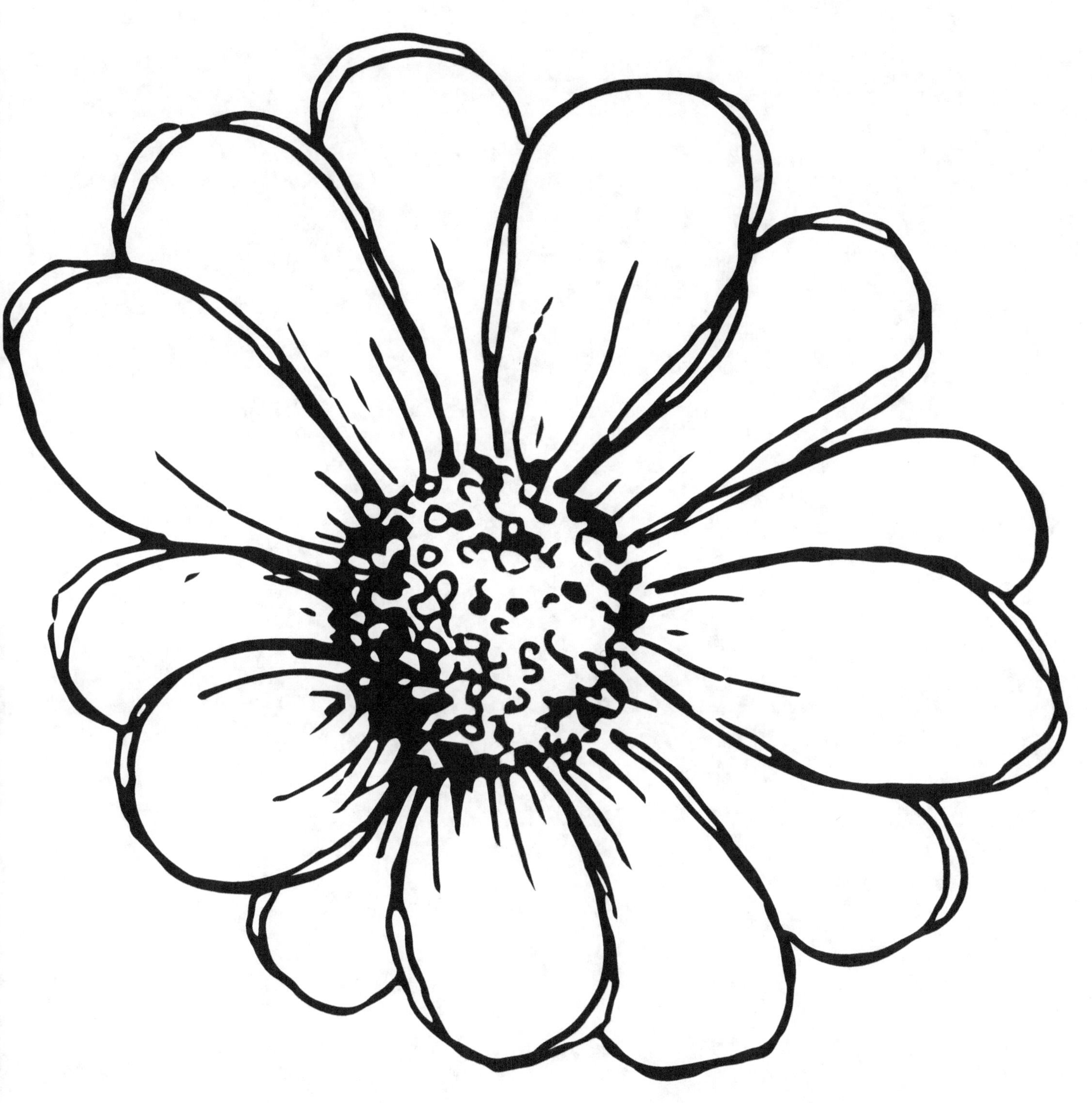

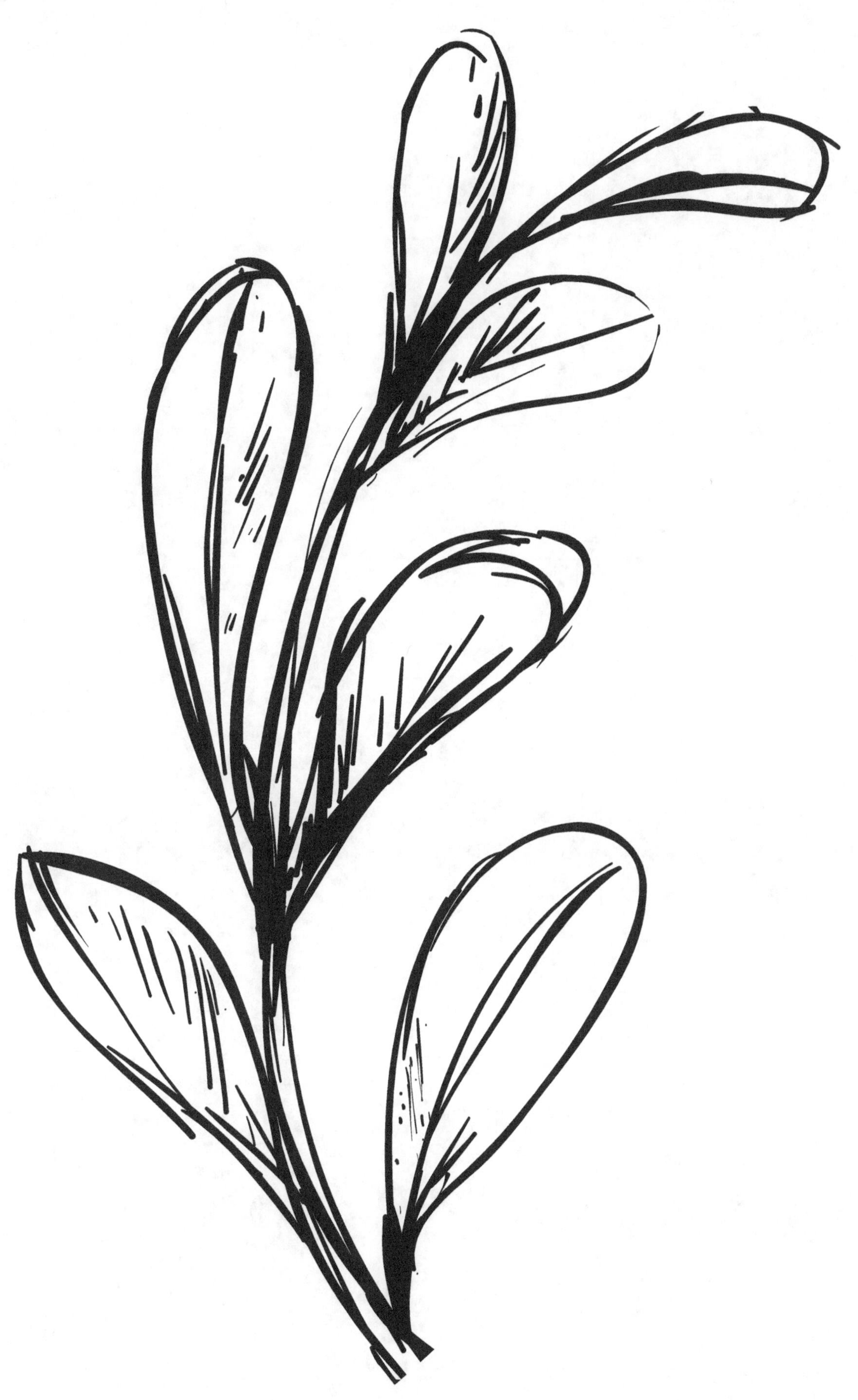

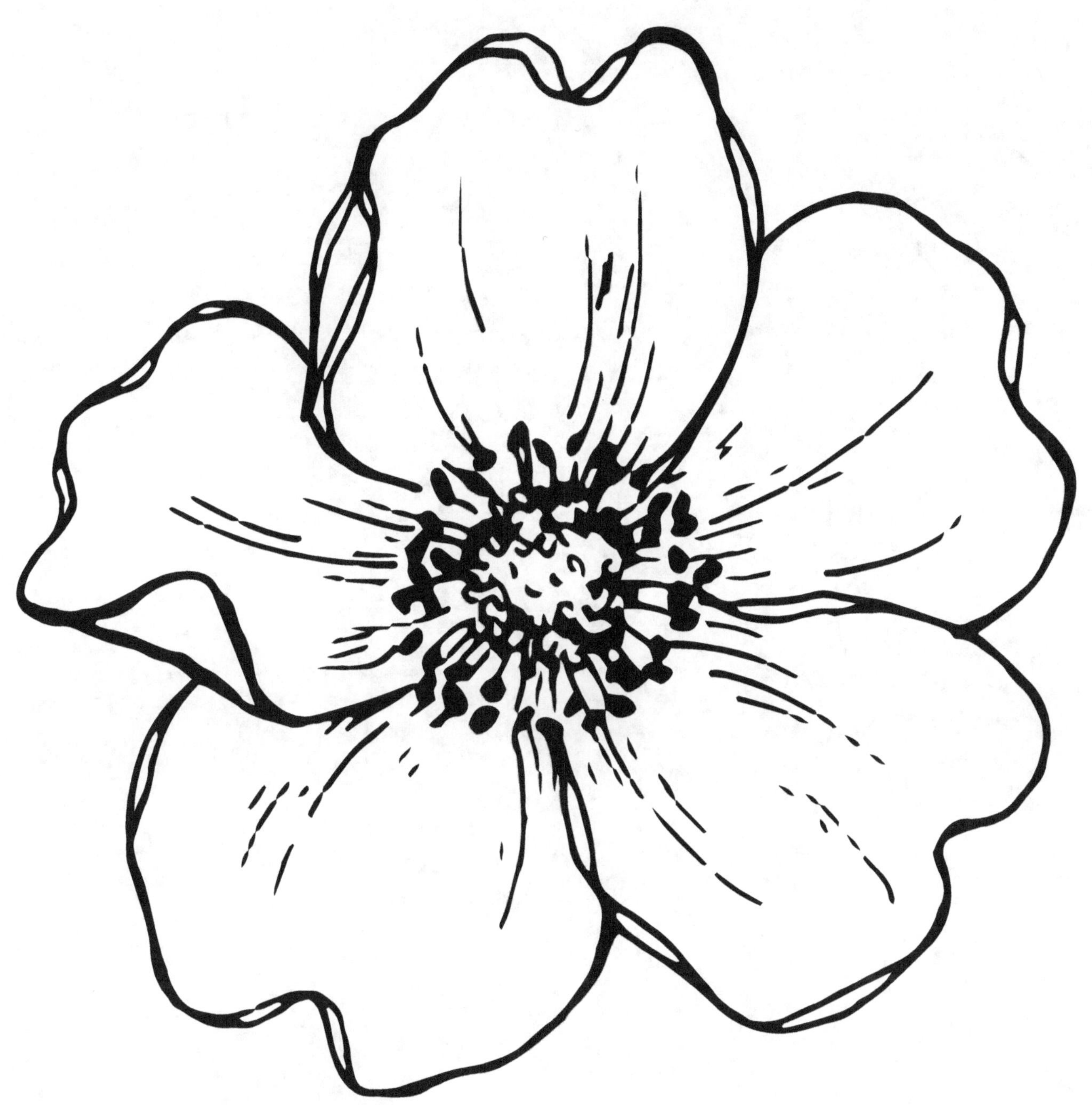

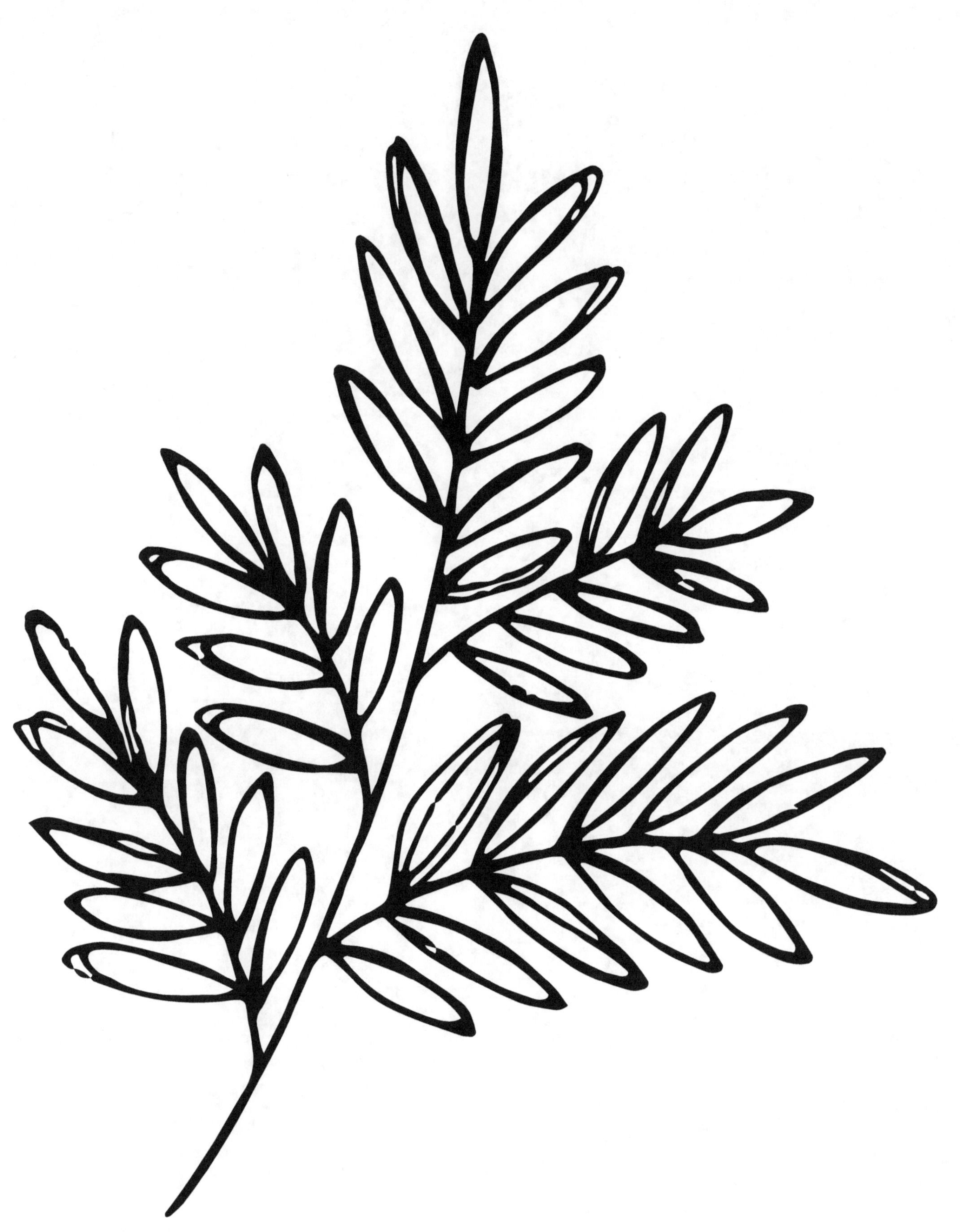

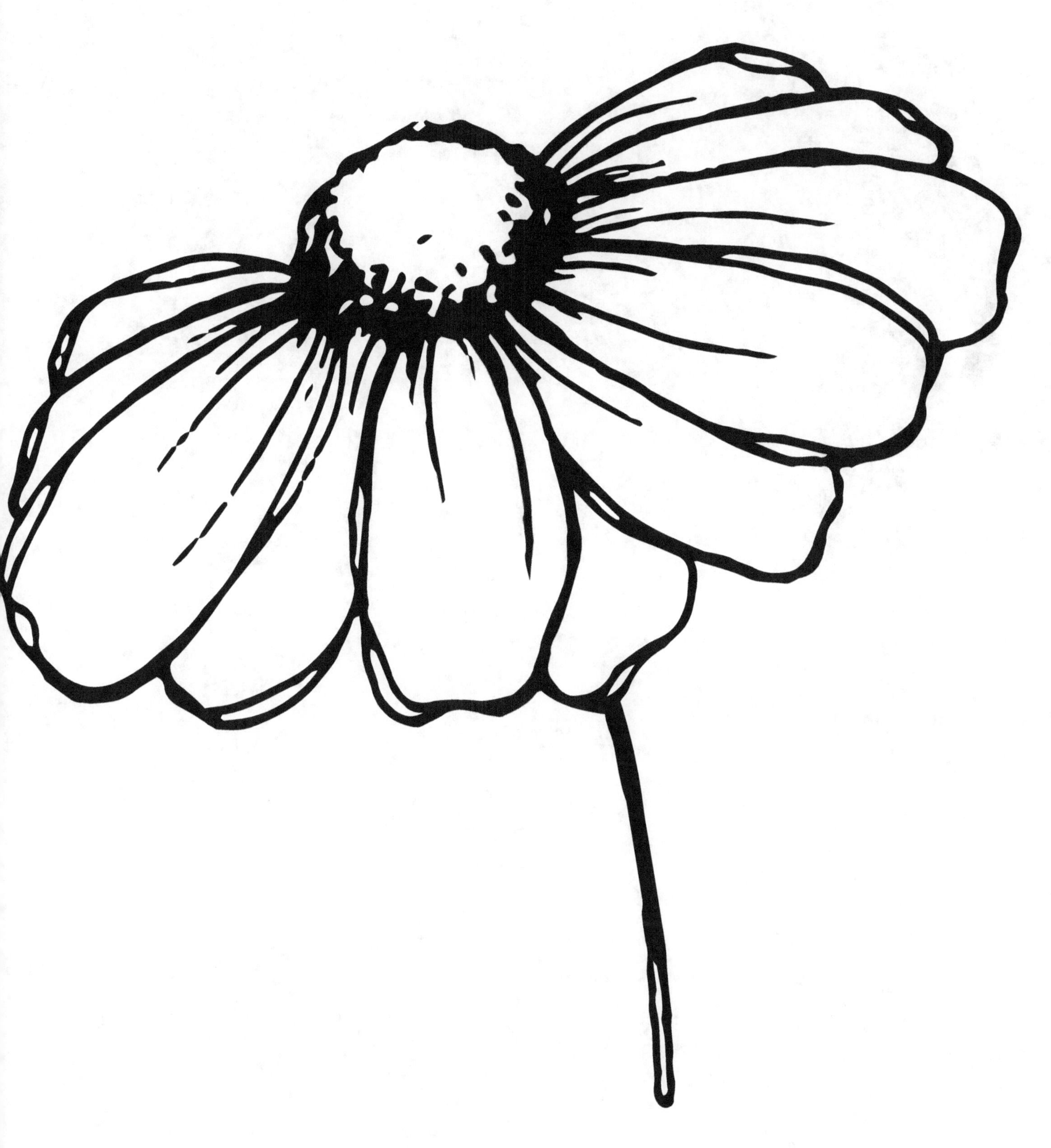

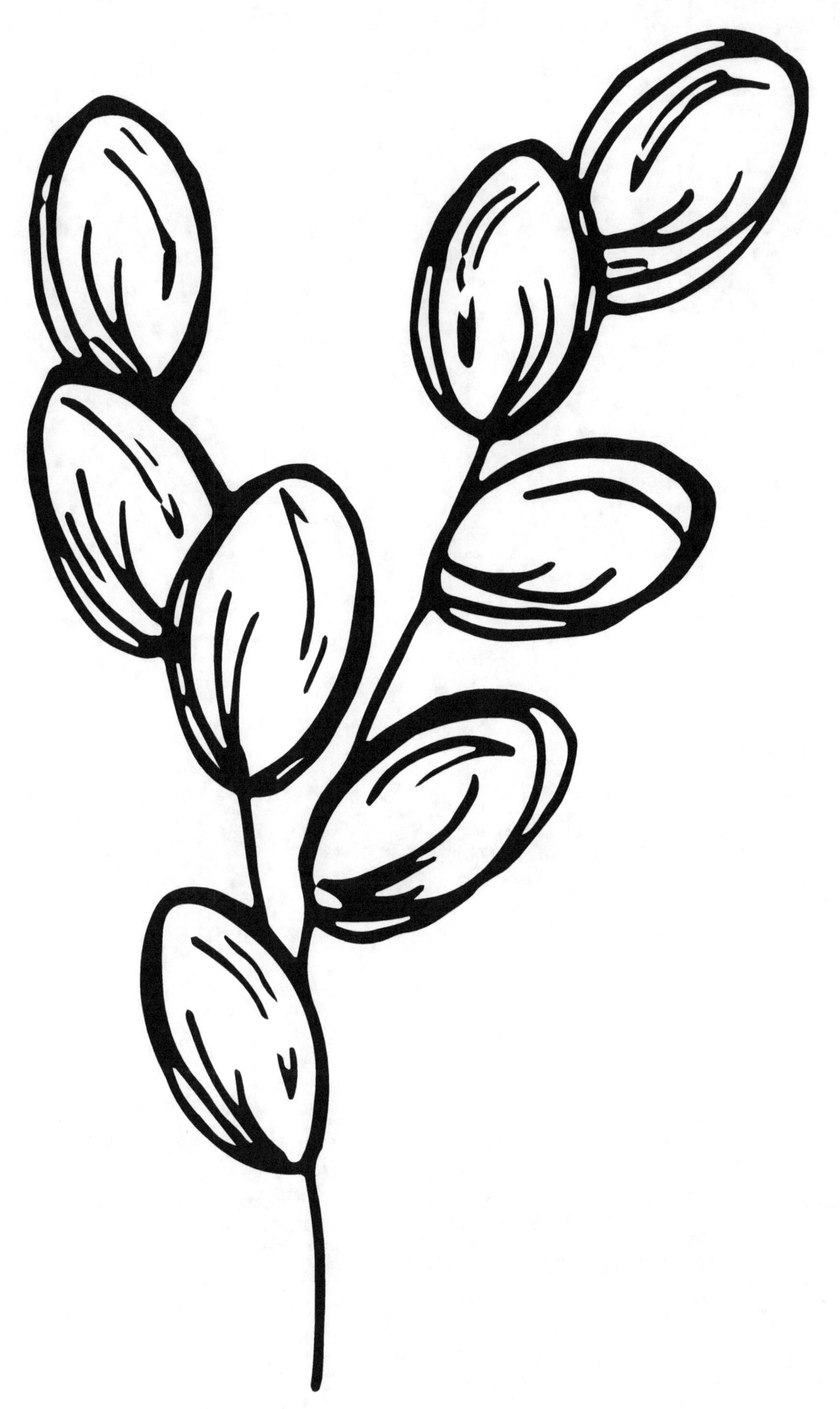

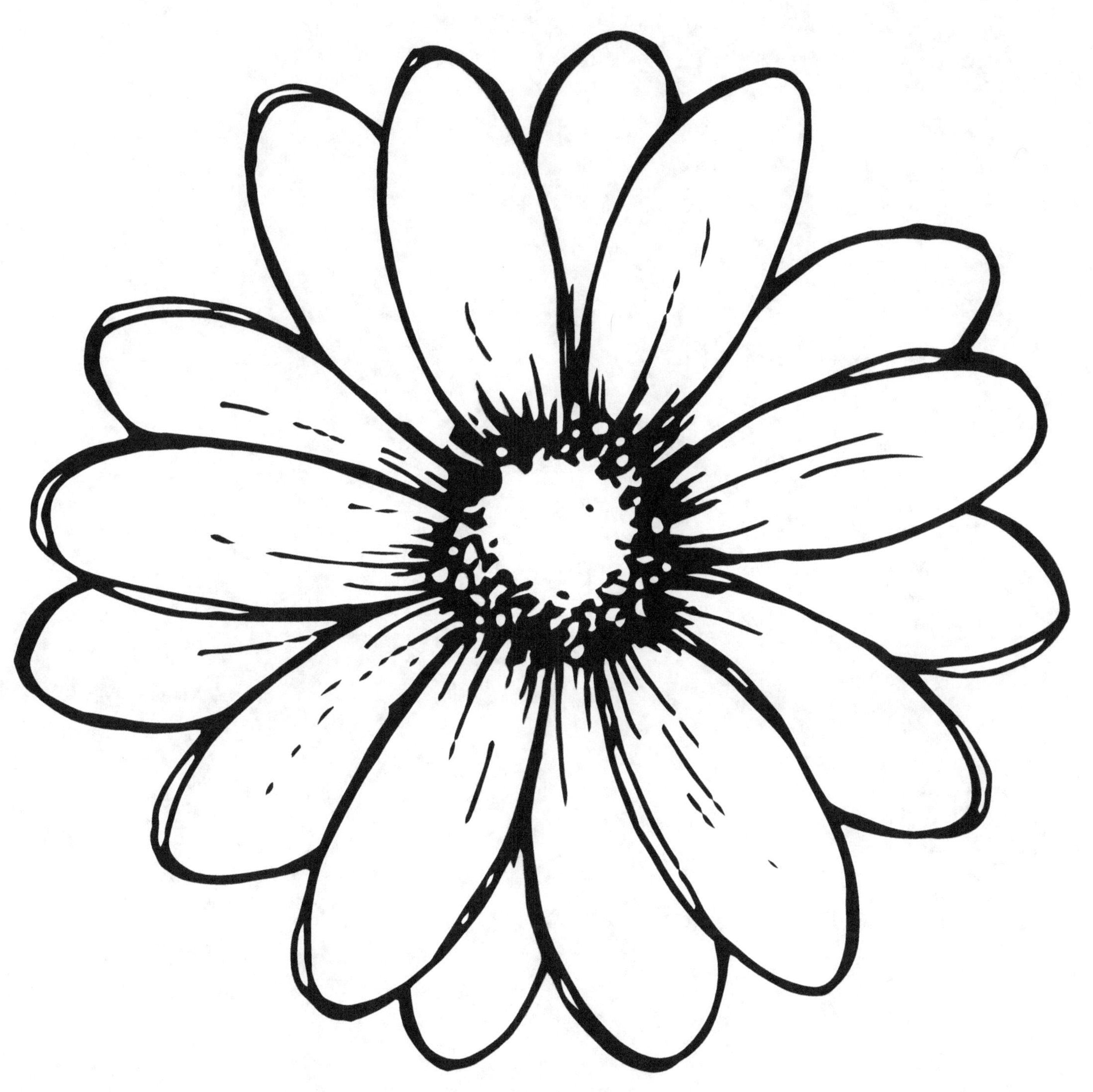

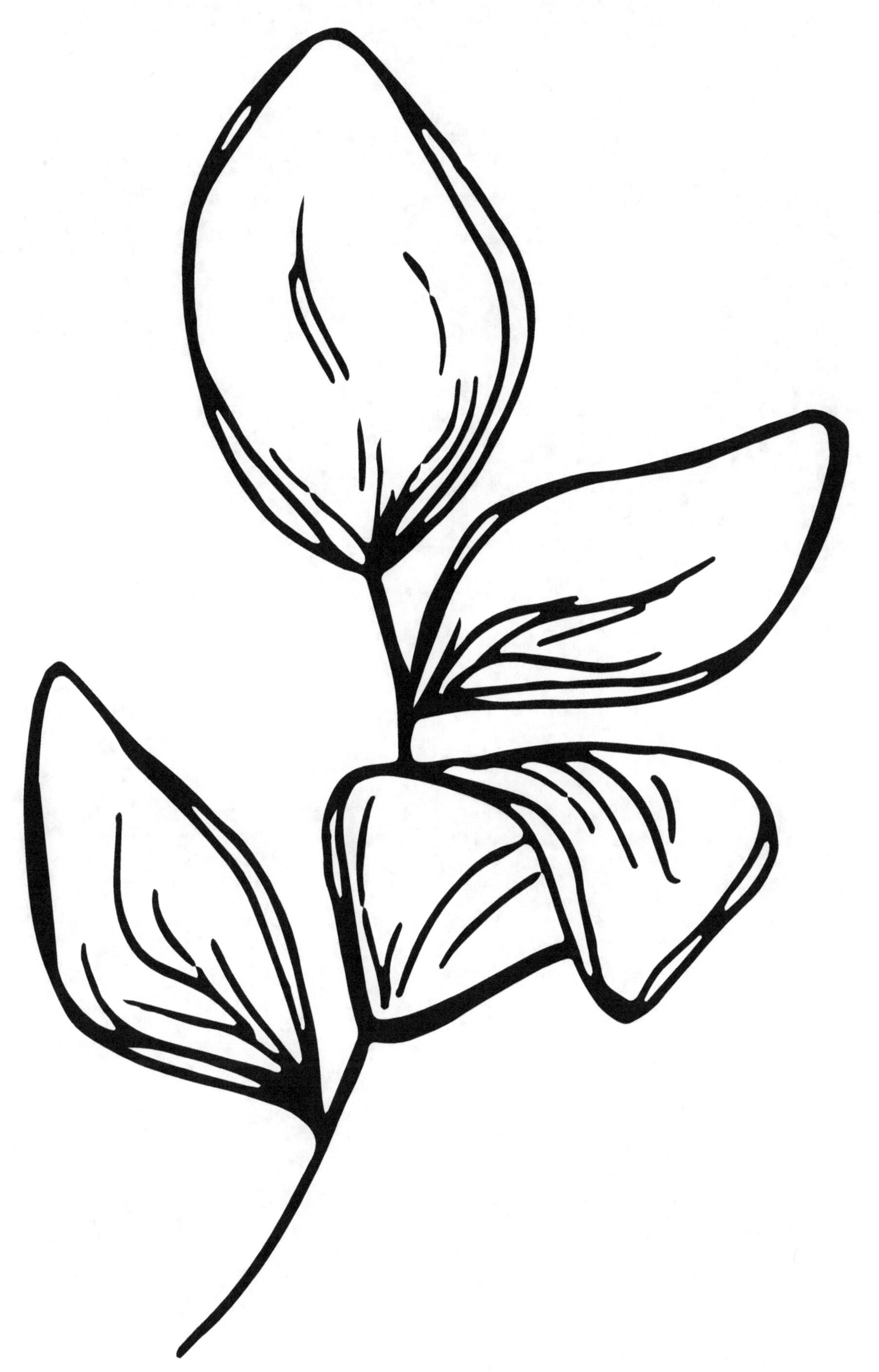

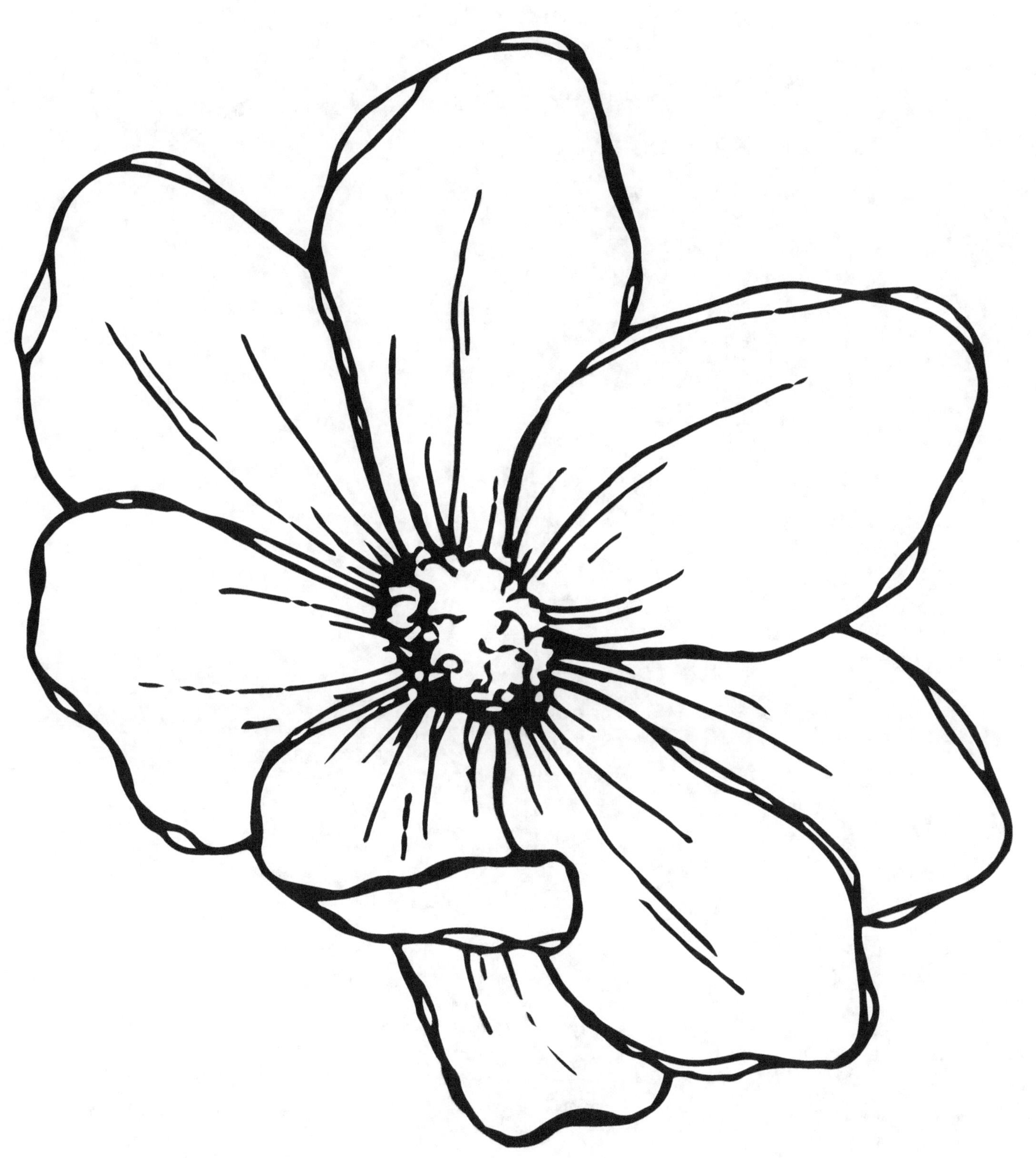

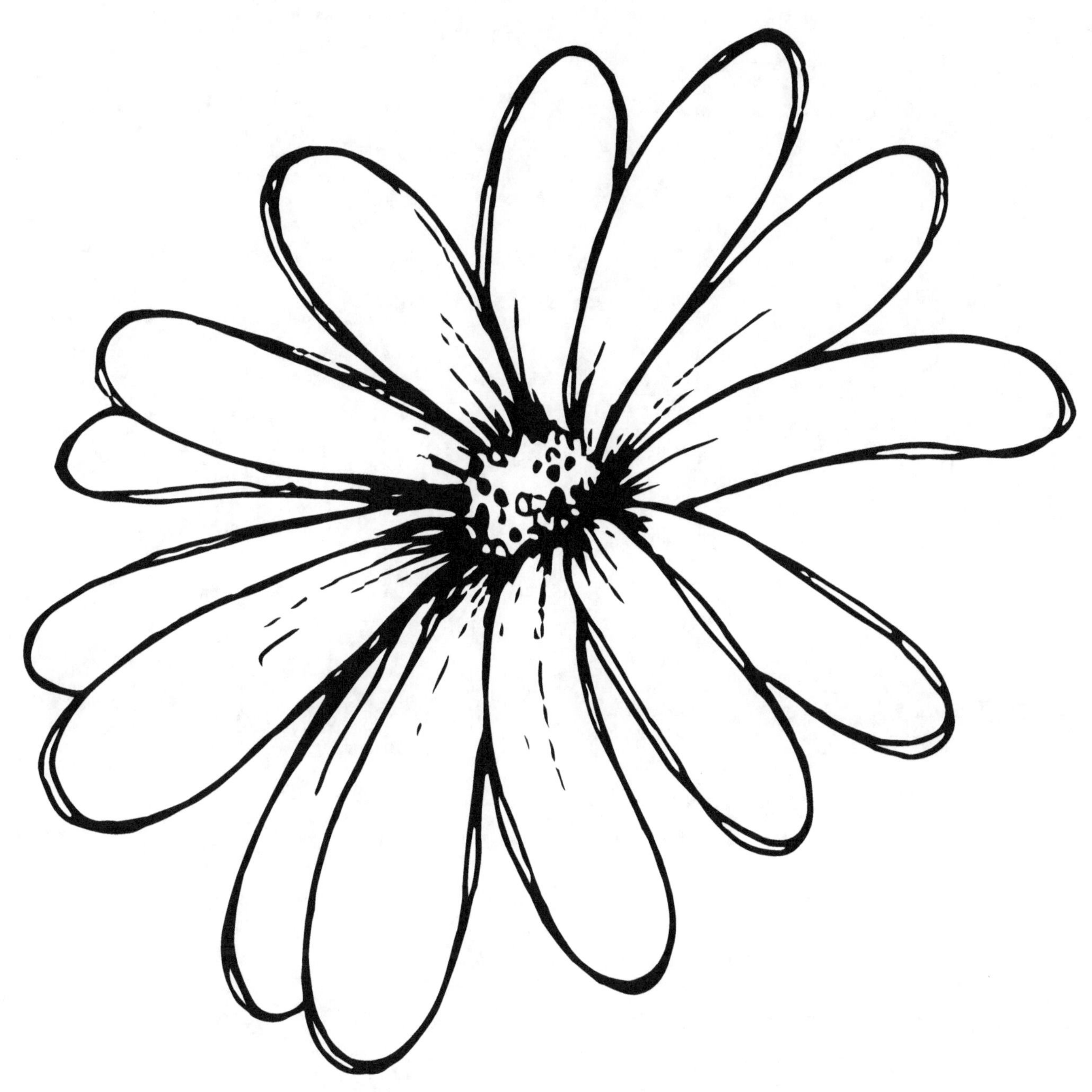

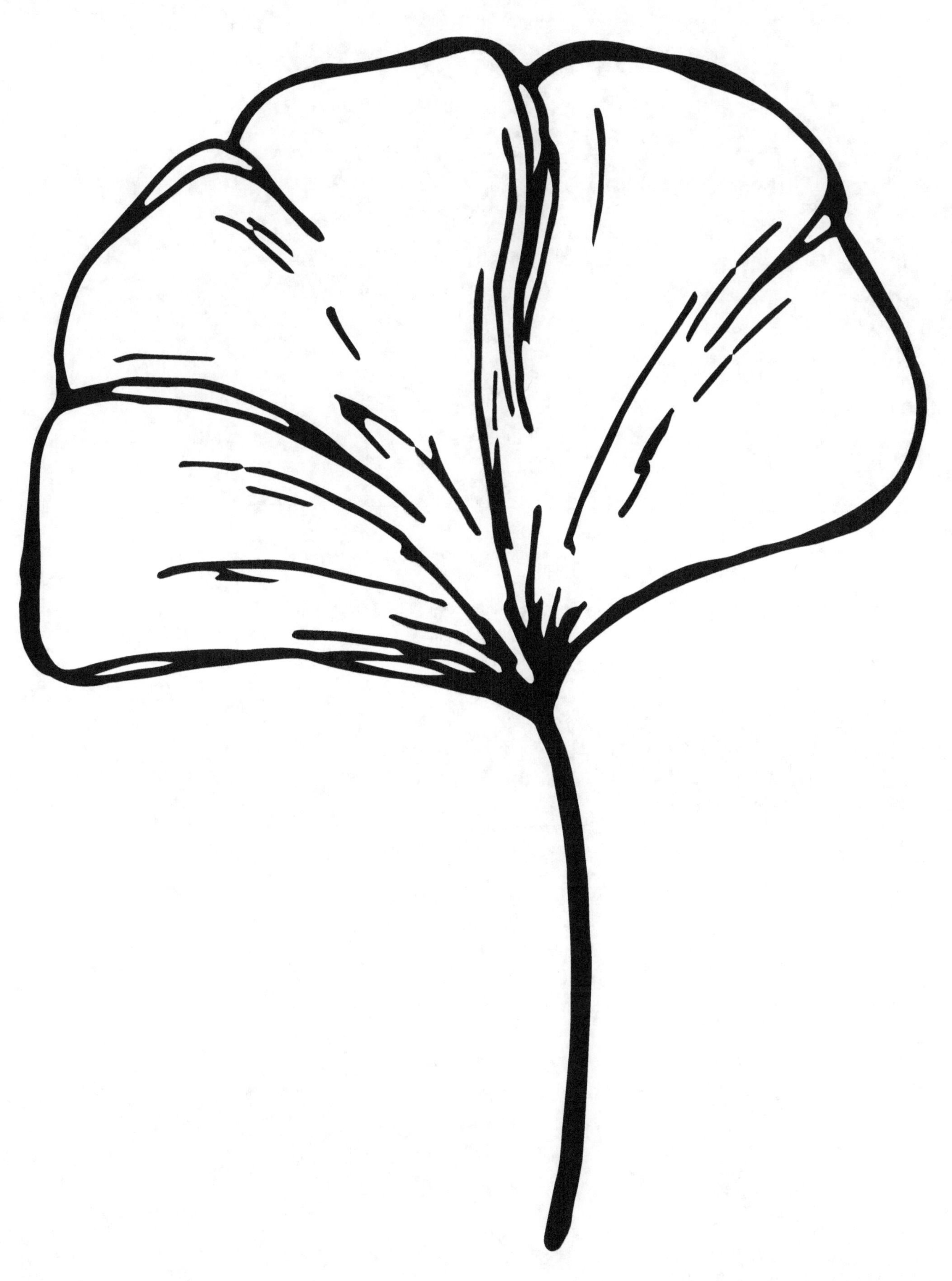

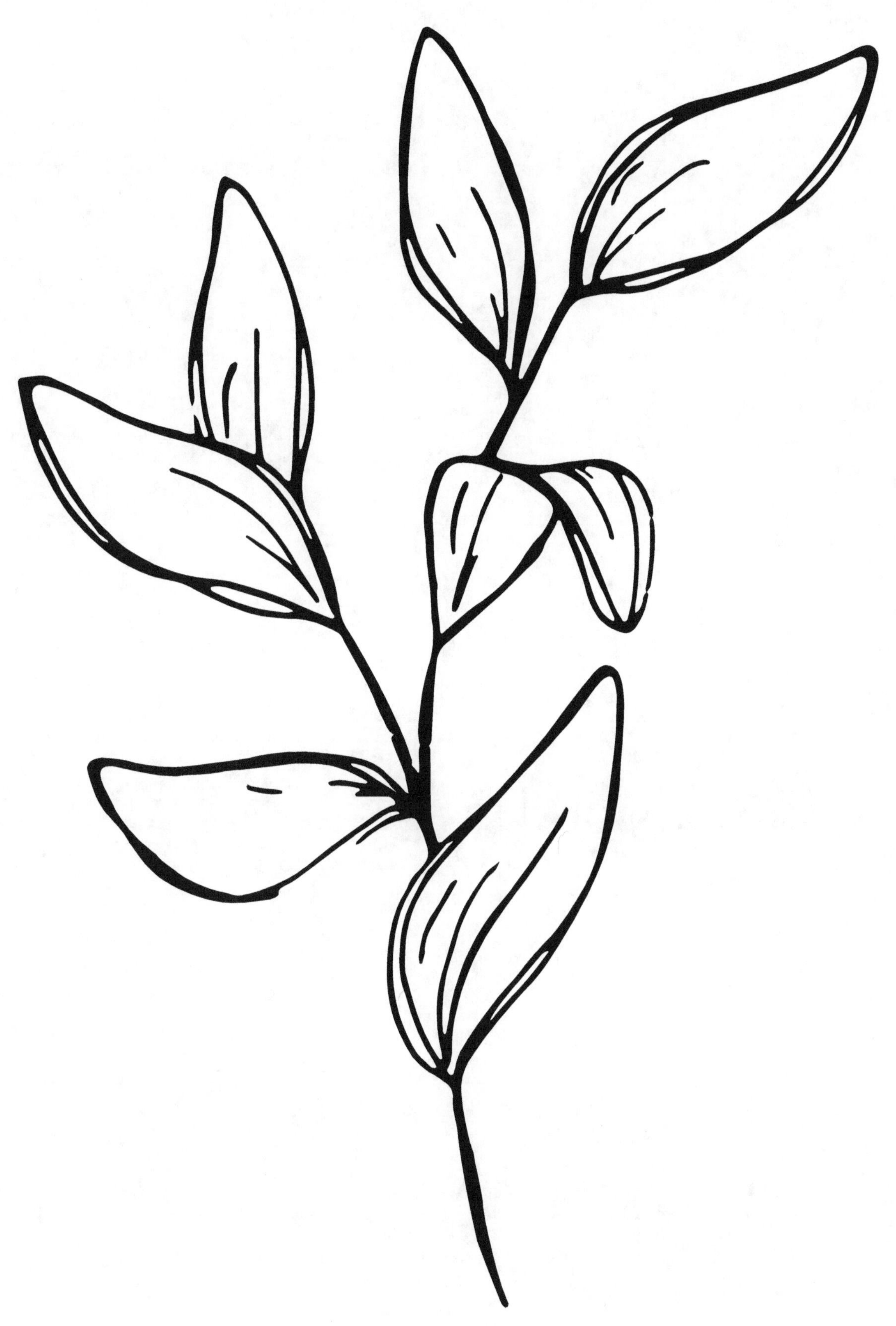

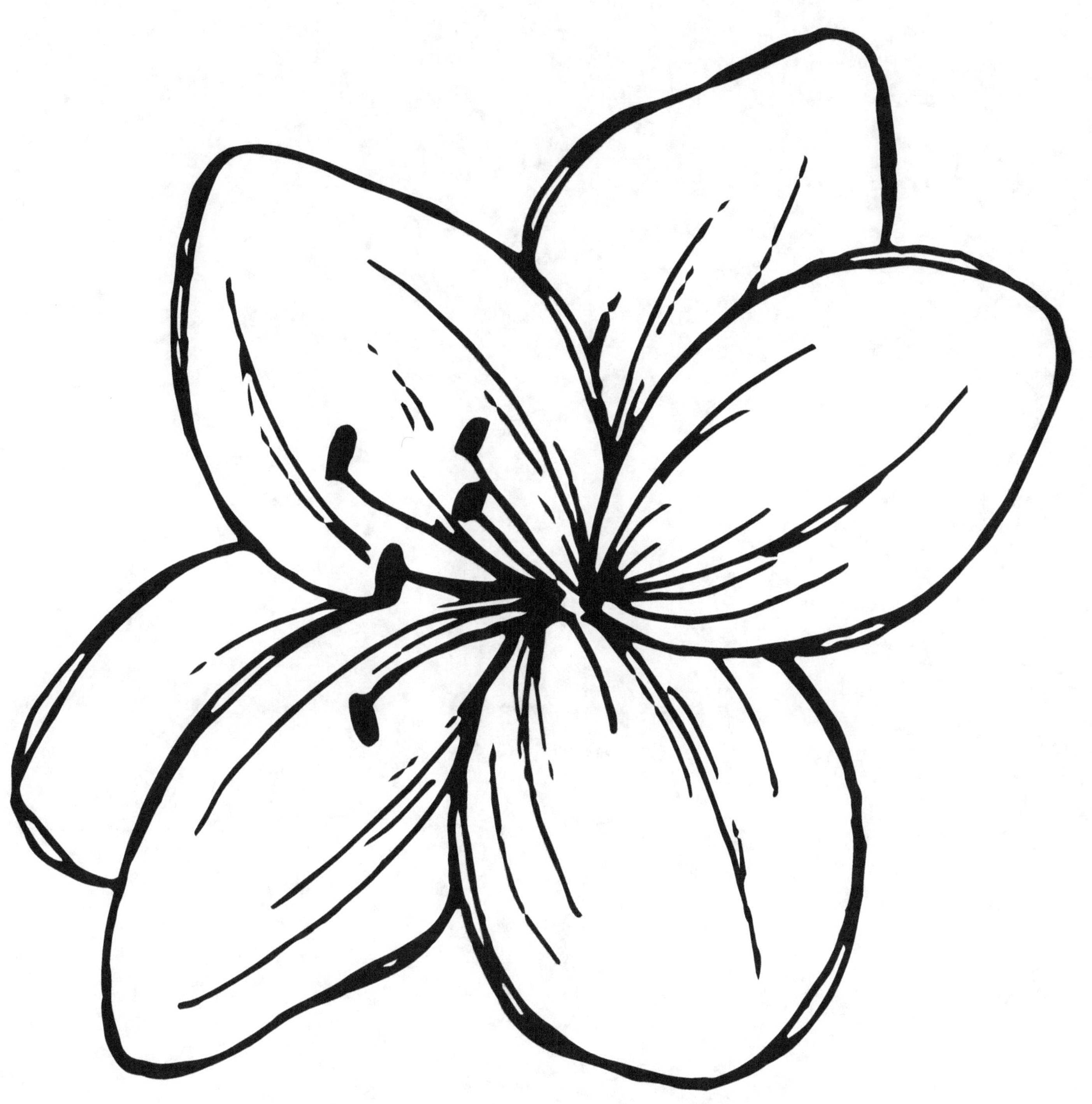

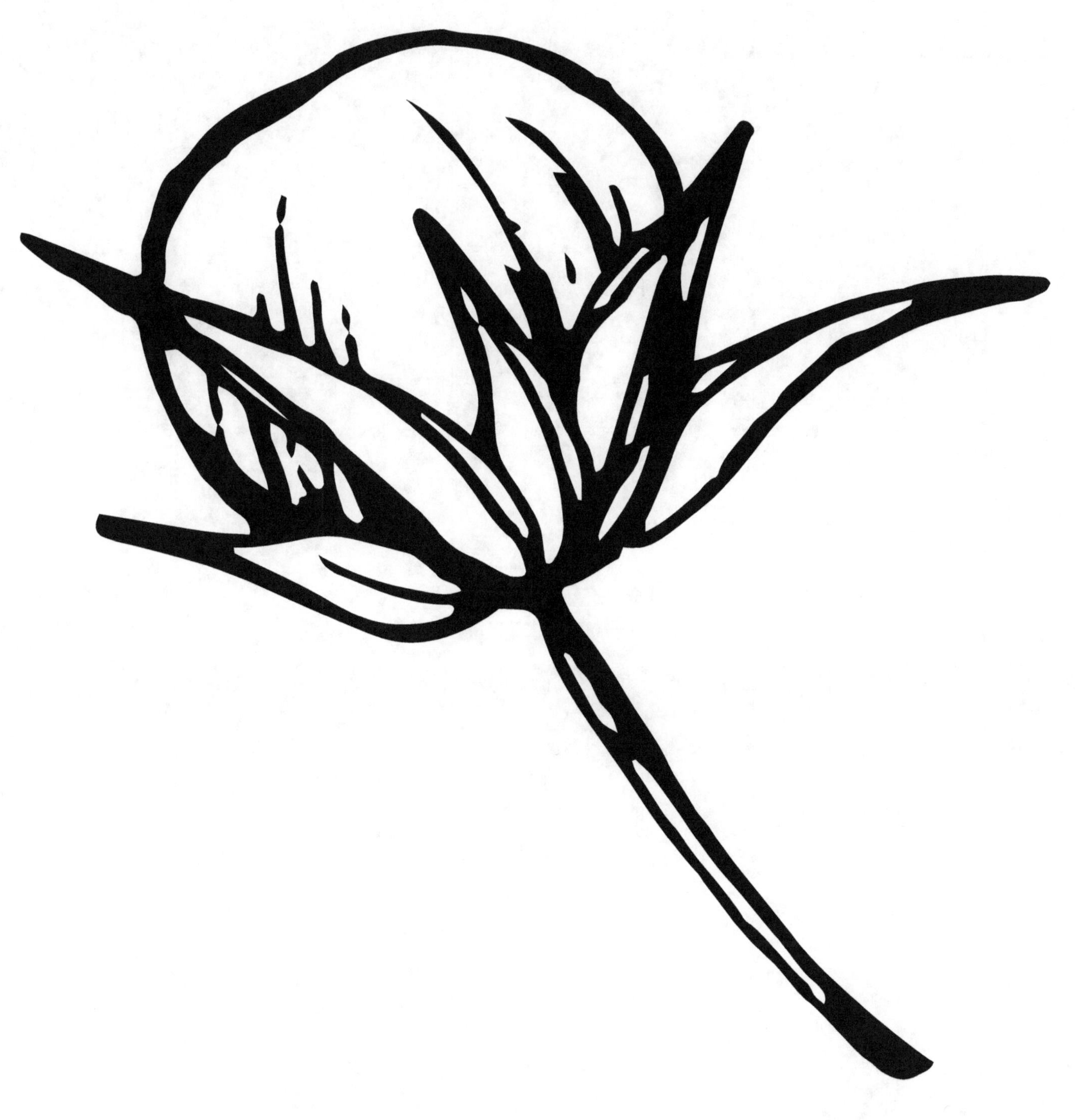

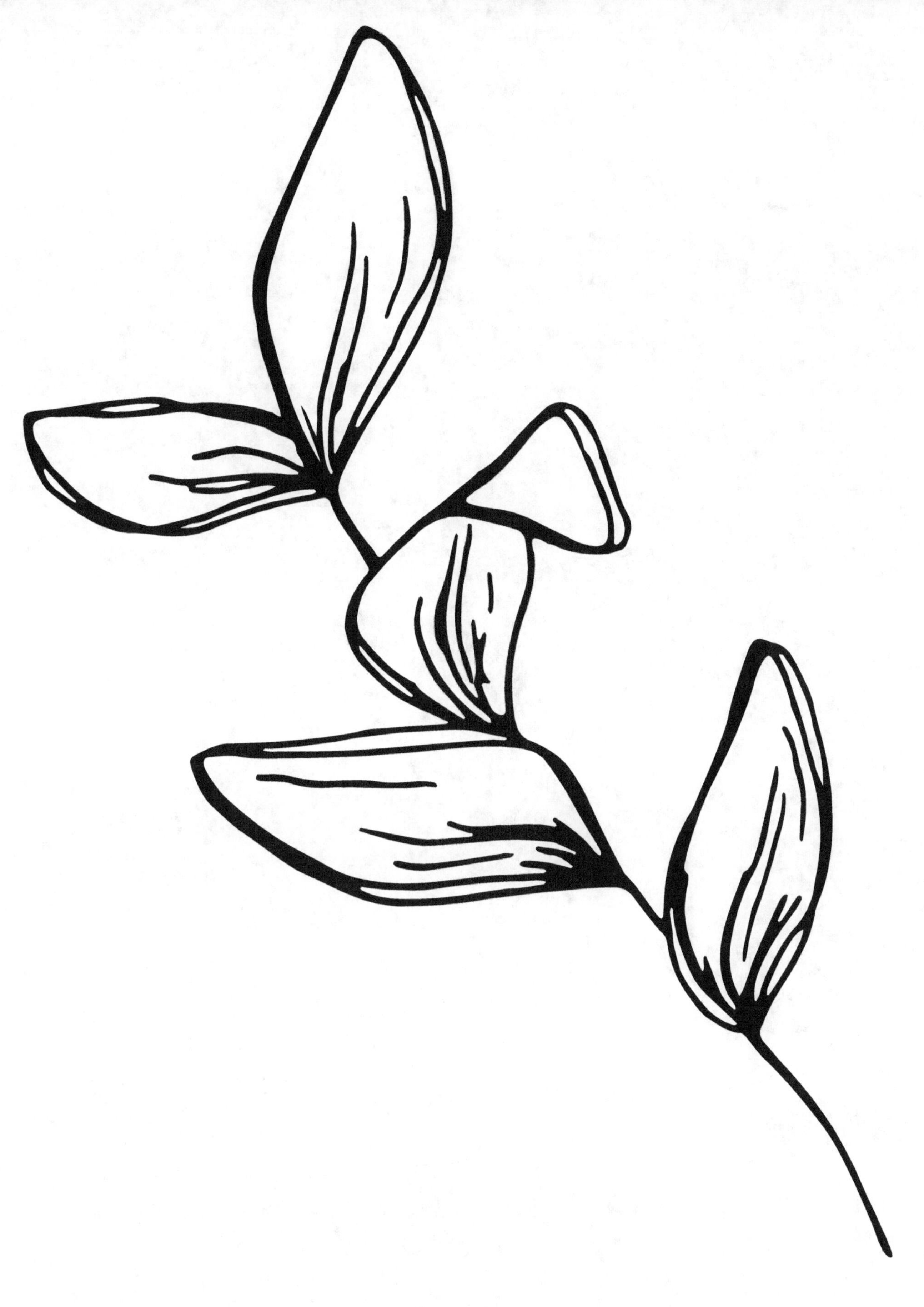

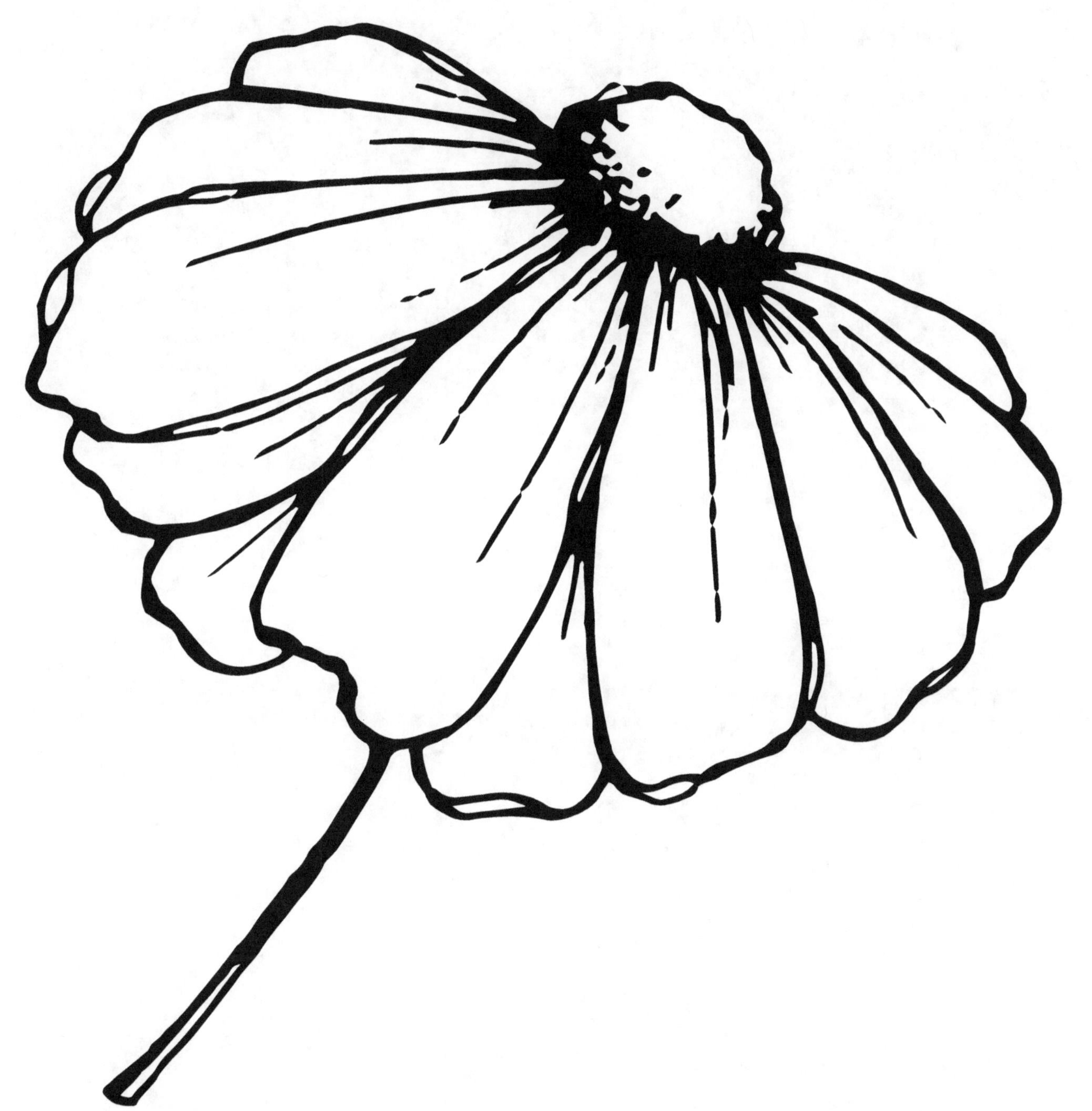

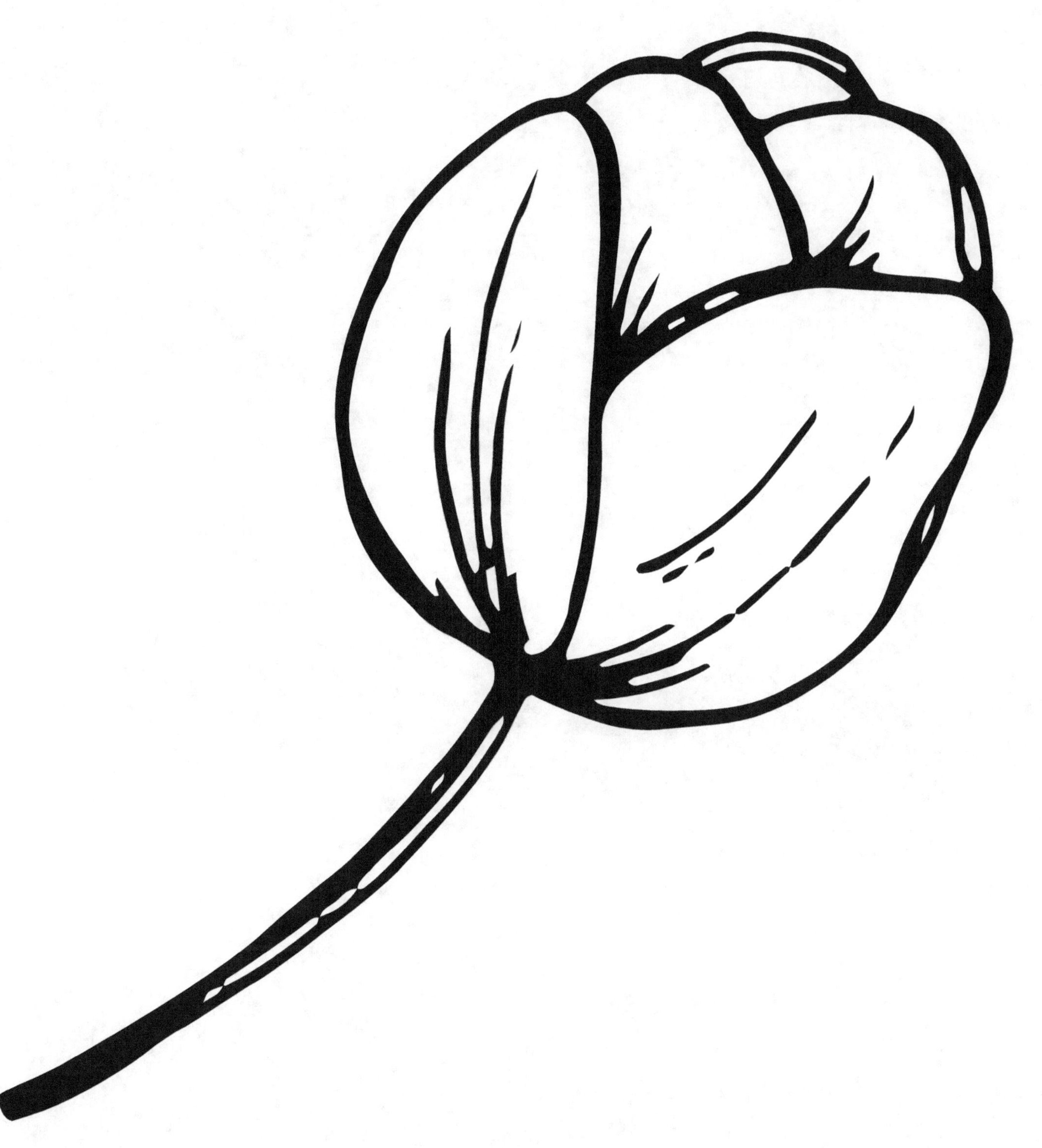

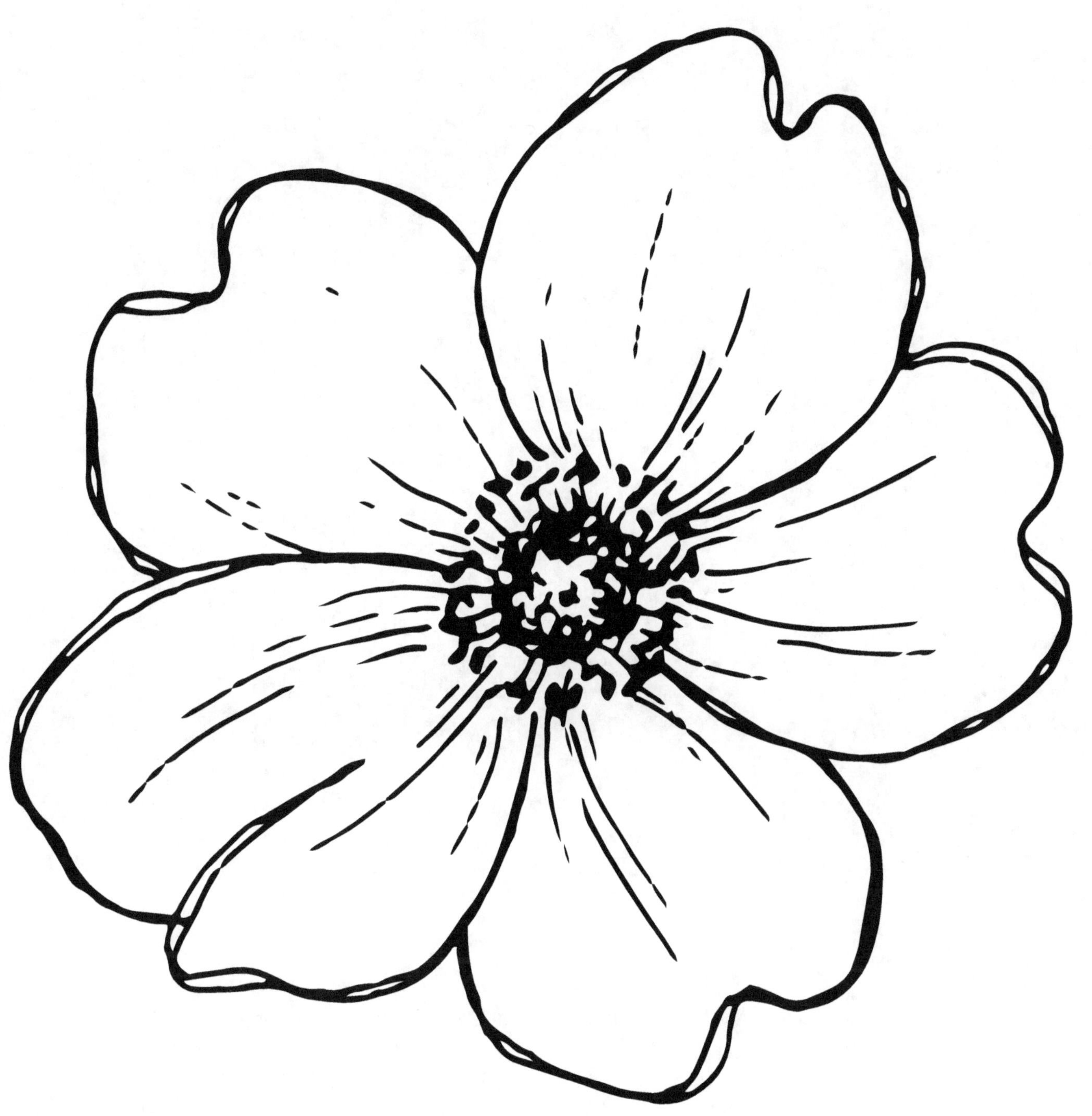

create
daily

BUILD THE LIFE OF
YOUR DREAMS